SCHOLASTIC

GRADE 5

Great Grammar Practice

Linda Ward Beech

D1296752

New York • Toronto • London • Auckland • Sydney
New Delhi • Mexico City • Hong Kong • Buenos Aires

Teaching *Resources*

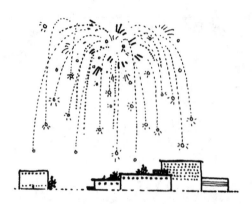

Edited by Mela Ottaiano
Cover design by Michelle Kim
Interior design by Melinda Belter

ISBN: 978-0-545-79425-1
Copyright © 2015 by Scholastic Inc.
Illustrations copyright © by Scholastic Inc.
All rights reserved.
Published by Scholastic Inc.
Printed in the U.S.A.

1 2 3 4 5 6 7 8 9 10   40   22 21 20 19 18 17 16 15

Contents

Introduction

To be successful at any task, it is important to have the right tools and skills. Grammar is one of the basic tools of written and oral language. Students need to learn and practice key grammar skills to communicate effectively. The pages in this book provide opportunities to introduce grammar rules and concepts and/or expand students' familiarity with them.

Using This Book

If your class has grammar texts, you can duplicate the pages in this book to use as reinforcement.

✏ Read aloud the instructions and examples as some of the material will be unfamiliar to fifth graders. If necessary, provide additional examples and answer students' questions.

✏ Model how to do the activity.

You can add these pages as assignments to your writing program and keep copies in skills folders at your writing resource center.

You may also want to use the activities as a class lesson or have students complete the pages in small groups.

Page by Page

You can use these suggestions to help students complete the activity pages.

Activity 1
Review what students know about subjects and predicates before introducing this page.

Activity 2
Point out that a complete subject might include adjectives, articles, and prepositional phrases.

Activity 3
Point out that a complete predicate might include adjectives, adverbs, articles, and prepositional phrases.

Activity 4
Use the chart to review the terms for each kind of sentence. Students may already be familiar with the terms *statement*, *question*, *command*, and *exclamation*.

Activity 5
Draw attention to questions in the exercises in which a helping verb is separated from the main verb by the subject.

Activity 6
Review what students know about sentence subjects before introducing this page.

Activity 7
Review what students know about subject-verb agreement before introducing this page. You might want to mention that *either/or* and *neither/nor* are called correlative conjunctions.

Activity 8
Make sure students understand they have to delete some words when they combine the two sentences in Part B.

Activity 9
Be sure students understand how a compound sentence differs from a compound subject or a compound predicate.

Activity 10
Run-on sentences are a common error in student writing. This page offers practice in identifying and correcting them.

Activity 11
Be sure students understand how a compound sentence differs from a compound subject or a compound predicate.

Activity 12

Review the difference between a concrete and an abstract noun.

Activity 13

Have students name other examples of common and proper nouns. For example: *street*, *lake*, *holiday*, and *organization*.

Activity 14

Suggest that students memorize the rules for forming plurals.

Activity 15

The placement of the apostrophe in possessive nouns is confusing to students, and they may need additional practice.

Activity 16

Point out that as in the example, pronouns don't always appear in the same sentence as the nouns they replace.

Activity 17

Before students begin the page, discuss what each subject pronoun represents. For example, *I* represents oneself and *we* represents oneself and one or more others.

Activity 18

The misuse of pronouns is common. Object pronouns are often misused as subjects. Give incorrect examples such as "Him and I are friends."

Activity 19

Review the chart with students before they begin the page.

Activity 20

Invite volunteers to share some of the proper nouns they wrote in Part A.

Activity 21

Point out that forms of the linking verb *to be* are the most commonly used verbs in the English language.

Activity 22

Review the object pronouns in Activity 18 before introducing this page. To determine if a verb has a direct object, suggest that students ask themselves "What?" after encountering a verb in a sentence. For example, "Glaciers move what?"

Activity 23

Have students make up their own examples of linking verbs followed by predicate nouns and predicate adjectives.

Activity 24

Subject-verb agreement is difficult for some students. You might do this page aloud with them so they can hear the correct usage and discuss why a verb is singular or plural.

Activity 25

When writing, students need to learn consistency in using verb tenses. In Part B, students should use the first verb in the sentence as the model.

Activity 26

Remind students that some helping verbs have singular and plural forms.

Activity 27

Forms of the verb *to do* are often misused. You might do this page aloud so students can hear the correct usage.

Activity 28

This page introduces principal verb parts that students should master.

Activity 29

This page introduces the perfect verb tenses. Explain that the present perfect tense also includes *have* for plural subjects. For example, "The students have picked a field trip destination."

Activity 30
Remind students that the subjects and verbs in sentences must agree and verb tenses should be consistent.

Activity 31
Mention that when a sentence has a linking verb, an adjective modifying the subject comes after the verb.

Activity 32
Before assigning this page, review what students know about proper nouns.

Activity 33
Mention that articles are also called noun markers because they indicate nouns. Have students memorize the rules for using articles.

Activity 34
Review the rules for using these adjectives before assigning the page.

Activity 35
Review what students already know about verbs and adverbs before assigning the page.

Activity 36
These words are often misused. Review what students know about adjectives and adverbs before assigning the page.

Activity 37
Invite volunteers to share the sentences they wrote in Part B.

Activity 38
Review what students know about object pronouns before assigning this page.

Activity 39
Explain that like adjectives and adverbs, prepositional phrases add more detail to a sentence.

Activities 40 and 41
Caution students not to overuse interjections in their writing.

Activity 42
Invite volunteers to share how they completed the sentences in Part A.

Activity 43
Before introducing the exercise, review what students know about capitalizing the first word of a sentence and proper names.

Activities 44 and 45
Explain that a comma is like a yellow traffic light for readers; it indicates a slight pause. When used in a series, commas help readers differentiate the items mentioned. Commas often appear in dialogue, after introductory phrases and nouns of address.

Activity 46
Review words that would not be capitalized in a title. For example: *in*, *of*, *to*, and *the*.

Activity 47
In the first example, point out that the quotation has its own end punctuation— a period—and it is placed within the quotation marks.

Activity 48
If necessary, review where to place quotation marks when writing dialogue and when punctuation should fall within quotation marks. You may also want to review which words in a title would not be capitalized and remind students to underline book or movie titles, but put quotation marks around a song title.

Activity 49
Learning the meanings of these words should help students know how to use and spell them correctly. Suggest that students make charts of easily confused words.

Activities 50 and 51
Suggest that students find and use other words spelled with these letters.

Great Grammar Practice, Grade 5 © 2015 by Scholastic Teaching Resources

Activities 52 and 53

Encourage students to find and use other words that begin with these prefixes and suffixes.

Activity 54

Invite volunteers to share how they determined the ranking of a synonym set.

Activity 55

Remind students that learning the meaning of these and other easily confused words will help them know how to use and spell them correctly.

Connections to the Standards

With the goal of providing students nationwide with a quality education that prepares them for college and careers, broad standards were developed to establish rigorous educational expectations. These standards serve as the basis of many state standards. The chart below details how the activities in this book align with specific language and foundational skills standards for students in grade 5.

	English Language Arts Standards	Activities
Language	**Conventions of Standard English**	
	• Demonstrate command of the conventions of standard English grammar and usage when writing or speaking.	1–55
	• Demonstrate command of the conventions of standard English capitalization, punctuation, and spelling when writing.	10, 13–15, 20, 32, 37, 41–55
	Knowledge of Language	
	• Use knowledge of language and its conventions when writing, speaking, reading, or listening.	1–55
	Vocabulary Acquisition and Use	
	• Determine or clarify the meaning of unknown and multiple-meaning words and phrases based on grade 5 reading and content, choosing flexibly from an array of strategies.	12, 14, 22, 33, 35, 41, 42, 44, 49–55
	• Demonstrate understanding of figurative language, word relationships, and nuances in word meanings.	1–55
	• Acquire and use accurately grade-appropriate general academic and domain-specific words and phrases, including those that signal contrast, addition, and other logical relationships.	1–55
Foundational Skills	**Phonics and Word Recognition**	
	• Know and apply grade-level phonics and word analysis skills in decoding words.	12, 14, 15, 32, 49–55
	Fluency	
	• Read with sufficient accuracy and fluency to support comprehension.	1–55

Name _____ Date _____

Focus on Sentences

A sentence is a group of words that expresses a complete idea.
The subject tells who or what the sentence is about.
The predicate tells what the subject does or is.

Four boys | found a cave in 1940.   **Lost their dog Robot.**

complete idea with subject and predicate   incomplete idea; not a sentence

A. Write *sentence* or *not a sentence* for each group of words.

1. Robot disappeared from view. _____

2. The boys couldn't find him anywhere. _____

3. Heard barking in the ground. _____

4. Discovered a large hole nearby. _____

5. The curious kids. _____

6. The dog sounded excited. _____

7. The boys climbed carefully into the hole. _____

8. They stumbled into a huge cave. _____

B. Draw a vertical line between the subject and the predicate in each sentence.

9. The boys stared in wonder at paintings of animals that covered the cave walls.

10. People painted the animals on the walls about 15,000 years ago.

11. This remarkable cave is in Lascaux, France.

12. The boys accidentally discovered an ancient wonder.

 Great Grammar Practice, Grade 5 © 2015 by Scholastic Teaching Resources

Name _____ Date _____

Simple and Complete Subjects

A sentence has a simple subject and a complete subject. The simple subject is a noun or pronoun that is the most important word in the subject. The complete subject includes all the words in the subject.

simple subject

Different kinds of homes provide shelter for people.

complete subject

Underline the complete subject in each sentence.
Circle the simple subject.

1. Some people live on the water in houseboats.

2. Tall buildings provide apartments in large cities.

3. The suburbs around cities are filled with rows of houses.

4. Retired people sometimes buy mobile homes.

5. These traveling homes can be very comfortable.

6. A few Lapp families in Arctic lands make tents from reindeer skins.

7. The Dayaks in Borneo build longhouses on stilts.

8. About 90 workers can live together on an oil rig.

9. Many kings and queens live in palaces.

10. Village houses in Africa are sometimes built of mud and straw.

11. A family with children sometimes builds a treehouse in the yard.

12. Common building materials are wood, brick, and concrete.

Great Grammar Practice, Grade 5 © 2015 by Scholastic Teaching Resources

Name _____ Date _____

Simple and Complete Predicates

A sentence has a simple predicate and a complete predicate.
A simple predicate is the verb, the most important word in the predicate.
A complete predicate includes all the words in the predicate.

simple predicate

Tamar saw a poster on the wall.

complete predicate

Underline the complete predicate in each sentence.
Circle the simple predicate.

1. Tamar asked her parents for a pet many times.

2. Her parents worried about a pet in the house.

3. Tamar spotted a poster about Adopt-a-Dog Month.

4. She showed the poster to her mother.

5. Many of Tamar's friends owned pets.

6. Derek kept a bowl full of goldfish.

7. Nina lived on a farm with horses and cows.

8. Mom suggested a trip to the local pound.

9. They could look at the dogs there.

10. Tamar wrapped her arms around her mother in a hug.

11. They drove to the pound the following day.

12. They found the perfect pet for the family.

Kinds of Sentences

A sentence may be declarative, interrogative, imperative, or exclamatory.

Kind of Sentence	End Punctuation	Example
A **declarative** sentence makes a statement.	Period	Ginger went up in a hot air balloon.
An **interrogative** sentence asks a question.	Question mark	Did she have fun?
An **imperative** sentence gives a command. The subject is understood as *you*.	Period or exclamation mark	Tell us about her experience.
An **exclamatory** sentence shows strong feeling.	Exclamation mark	What a great time we had!

Read the sentences. Write *declarative, interrogative, imperative,* or *exclamatory*.

1. Have you ever ridden in a hot air balloon?   _____

2. Ask Ginger for a description.   _____

3. The noise is deafening and unpleasant.   _____

4. You're kidding!   _____

5. Riding over the treetops is an amazing experience.   _____

6. How long was the ride?   _____

7. What an adventure you had!   _____

8. Does a hot air balloon ever get stuck in the trees?   _____

9. How does the balloon move?   _____

10. Ask Mr. Cook for a demonstration.   _____

11. Great idea!   _____

Inverted Order

The subject usually comes before the predicate in a sentence. However, sometimes the order is inverted, and the subject comes after the predicate.

> **Regular Order:** We grow raspberries in the garden.

> **Inverted Order:** In the garden are the raspberries.

An interrogative sentence is inverted because all or part of the predicate comes before the subject.

> Do the raspberries taste good?

(part of predicate before subject)   (part of predicate after subject)

A. Write *regular* or *inverted* to identify the order of each sentence.

1. Through the field ran a female deer.   _____

2. Running beside her was a young one.   _____

3. Were they heading toward the raspberries?   _____

4. Can you see these luscious berries from the field?   _____

5. The deer can find everything edible on the property.   _____

6. Will Hassan help us pick the berries today?   _____

7. He has promised several hours of his time.   _____

8. On the table are the baskets for the berries.   _____

B. Circle the simple subject and underline the simple predicate in each sentence.

9. Are other deer hiding in the woods?

10. Out from the trees step three more hungry deer.

11. Dad has fenced in the raspberry patch.

Compound Subjects

A compound subject has two or more nouns or pronouns with the same predicate. The conjunction *and* joins the subjects. A compound subject agrees in number with the verb.

Adele and Bert write articles about food.

(two subjects joined by *and*)   (plural verb form)

A. Write *compound* or *not compound* to describe the subject in each sentence.

1. Diners and chefs read the articles. _____

2. Restaurants follow Adele and Bert's column, too. _____

3. A new article describes the ingredients in a curry dish. _____

4. Ginger and cumin are two of the spices in this dish. _____

5. Bert and his partner eat in many restaurants. _____

6. Adele tries a bite of all the appetizers, and Bert eats dessert samples. _____

7. The writers and their guests share the main courses. _____

B. Write the correct verb for each sentence.

8. The soup and salad _____ delicious at The Stone Café.
       taste   tastes

9. This restaurant _____ ten kinds of pizza.
       boast   boasts

10. Adele and her guests _____ very full.
       get   gets

Name _____ Date _____

Using *Either/Or* and *Neither/Nor*

Some compound subjects are joined by conjunction pairs. These are *either* and *or* and *neither* and *nor*. When these conjunctions are used, the verb in the sentence agrees with the subject closer to it.

Either the singers or the dancer is rehearsing.

singular noun ⬆ singular verb ⬆

Neither Mr. Bell nor his assistants are here.

plural noun ⬆ plural verb ⬆

Write the correct verb for each sentence.

1. Either Jesi or Betty _____ on the stage.

stand   stands

2. Neither the director nor the actors _____ ready.

is   are

3. Neither Patty nor her classmates _____ a script.

has   have

4. Either Arden or we _____ in charge of props.

is   are

5. Either the playwright or her agent _____ the school.

is visiting   are visiting

6. Neither the singers nor the actors _____ their parts.

is learning   are learning

7. Either Dale or the twins _____ scenery.

is making   are making

8. Either Honey or Will _____ costumes twice.

changes   change

Name _____ Date _____

Compound Predicates

A compound predicate has two verbs with the same subject.
The conjunction *and* joins the verbs.

The wind howled and raged. Joel opened the window and peered into the night.

verbs joined by *and*   verbs joined by *and*

A. Write *compound* or *not compound* to describe the predicate in each sentence.

1. Snow fell and drifted across the field. _____

2. The storm continued throughout the night. _____

3. In the house the temperature dropped,
and the furnace went on. _____

4. Joel shivered and returned to his bed. _____

5. The alarm clock rang early and woke him. _____

6. Mom and Dad made a hearty breakfast. _____

7. Joel jumped out of bed and dressed quickly. _____

B. Combine each pair of sentences to make a sentence with a compound predicate.

8. Dad waxed the skis. He checked the bindings.

_____

9. They crossed the white field. They skied into the nearby woods.

_____

10. The snow crunched under their skis. The snow sparkled in the sun.

_____

Name _____ Date _____

Simple and Compound Sentences

A simple sentence contains a complete subject and a complete predicate. A compound sentence contains two simple sentences joined by a comma and a linking word called a conjunction.

Conjunction	Purpose	Example
and	connects two related ideas	Traffic is slow in the city, <u>and</u> it almost stops at rush hour.
but	connects ideas that differ or shows a problem with first idea	Verna likes buses, <u>but</u> she walks during rush hour.
or	suggests a choice of ideas	Many workers take the subway, <u>or</u> they take a bus.

Write *simple* or *compound* to identify each sentence.

1. A bus travels in the right lane, and taxis pass in the left lane. _____

2. Men and women wait at the bus stop. _____

3. People on bicycles stop and go along with the other traffic. _____

4. Two shoppers look for a cab, but there are none available. _____

5. Students burst out of school, and they head for their buses. _____

6. Workers dash for trains, or they stay late at their offices. _____

7. Some people are in a hurry, but they may have to wait. _____

8. Most people catch the train, but some people miss it. _____

9. Pedestrians fill the sidewalks, and children on scooters add to the crowds. _____

10. Dog walkers head to the park now, or they can wait until later. _____

Run-on Sentences

> A run-on sentence has too many ideas that run together without the correct punctuation.
>
> **Run-on Sentence:** Many kids are on sports teams the teams practice after school.
>
> **New Sentences:** Many kids are on sports teams.
> The teams practice after school.

A. Write *run-on* or *sentence* next to each group of words.

1. Soccer players use their feet to move the ball.   _____

2. The swimmers are working out our pool is indoors.   _____

3. The coach is here where are the players?   _____

4. The pitchers throws the ball the batter misses.   _____

5. The batter hits the ball and runs to first base.   _____

B. Write two sentences for each run-on sentence below.

6. Use a racket to hit a tennis ball the ball goes over the net.

_____

7. Runners do laps around the field the track meet is next weekend.

_____

8. The bus arrives from the other school now the meet can begin.

_____

9. The runners cross the finish line Jenna finished first.

_____

Name _____ Date _____

Review: Sentences

A simple sentence contains a complete subject and a complete predicate. Both the subject and predicate can be in compound form.

Simple Sentence With a Compound Subject: My brother and I like the Fourth of July.

Simple Sentence With a Compound Predicate: We go to a picnic and watch fireworks.

A compound sentence contains two simple sentences joined by a comma and a conjunction such as *and*, *or*, or *but*.

Compound Sentence: It is finally dark, and the fireworks can begin!

Write *compound subject*, *compound predicate*, or *compound sentence* to describe each sentence.

1. Mom and Dad took us to the town picnic. _____

2. We all wanted to find the food and start eating. _____

3. I chose a hot dog, but my brother wanted a hamburger. _____

4. We returned to our picnic blanket and got comfortable. _____

5. Mom waved to neighbors, and they came over to sit with us. _____

6. During the fireworks, my brother and I watched in amazement. _____

Name _____ Date _____

Focus on Nouns

A noun is a word that names a person, place, thing, or idea. A concrete noun names persons, places, and things that you can see and touch. An abstract noun names ideas and feelings that you cannot see.

Concrete: I saw a <u>sweater</u> in the <u>store</u>.

Abstract: I looked at it with <u>hope</u>.

A. Write the words from the word bank under the correct heading.

WORD BANK

laziness   socks   belt   sweetness   scarf   fame
musician   clerk   pain   confidence   shirt   bravery

Concrete Nouns	Abstract Nouns
1. _____	7. _____
2. _____	8. _____
3. _____	9. _____
4. _____	10. _____
5. _____	11. _____
6. _____	12. _____

B. Circle the nouns in each sentence.

13. Anna needed new clothes for the winter.

14. She went to the mall with her father to look for a warm jacket.

15. It was a pleasure to shop for jeans and tops.

16. With great excitement, Anna found the boots she wanted.

Proper Nouns

	Common Nouns	Proper Nouns
Nouns that name a particular person, place, or thing are proper nouns. They begin with a capital letter. All other nouns are common nouns.	person	Toby Smith, Aunt Gertrude
	state	Florida
	nation	Thailand
	month	February
	geographical body	Blue Ridge Mountains
	event	Olympics
	day	Saturday

A. Underline the common nouns and circle the proper nouns in each sentence.

   1. Mateo Garcia was called to serve on a jury in October.

   2. It was a busy time for the courts in Greenville.

   3. Prosecutors, lawyers, and witnesses came and went from the court.

   4. Judge Coretta Kent was presiding that Monday.

   5. The administrator asked some jurors to return in November.

   6. Moses Young borrowed a pen from his neighbor to fill out the forms.

B. Decide if each word is a common noun or a proper noun.
    Rewrite each proper noun correctly.

   7. associate _____

   8. officer wilson _____

   9. eastview school _____

   10. lake michigan _____

   11. indonesia _____

   12. recess _____

   13. attorney _____

   14. mount etna _____

   15. minneapolis _____

   16. allegheny river _____

Plural Nouns

Plural nouns name more than one person, place, or thing.
Most plural nouns end in -s. Other plural nouns follow special rules.

Rules	Examples
Add -es to nouns that end in x, z, ch, sh, s, or ss	foxes, bushes, patches
Add -s to nouns that end with a vowel plus y	boys, keys
For nouns ending with a consonant plus y, change the y to i, and add -es	spies, parties
For most nouns ending in f or fe, change the f or fe to v, and add -es	halves, lives
Add -s to most nouns that end with a vowel plus o	patios, radios
For some nouns ending in a consonant plus o, add -s or -es	silos, tomatoes

Write the plural form for each noun. Use a dictionary to help you.

1. essay _____

2. lady _____

3. leaf _____

4. studio _____

5. wolf _____

6. church _____

7. agency _____

8. wish _____

9. buzz _____

10. circus _____

11. class _____

12. hero _____

13. monkey _____

14. calf _____

15. dish _____

16. lunch _____

17. glass _____

18. wax _____

Name _____ Date _____

Possessive Nouns

A possessive noun shows ownership. A singular noun ends with an apostrophe and *s* (*'s*). A plural noun ends with *s* and an apostrophe (*s'*). Irregular plural nouns end with an apostrophe and *s* (*'s*).

Singular Possessive Noun	Plural Possessive Noun
teacher's lesson	teachers' lesson
class's play	classes' play
child's game	children's game

A. Write the possessive form for each underlined noun.

1. the <u>dog</u> tail _____

2. the <u>children</u> pony _____

3. <u>Thomas</u> cat _____

4. the <u>pigs</u> tails _____

5. that <u>spider</u> web _____

6. the <u>bees</u> honey _____

7. four <u>hens</u> feathers _____

8. the <u>sheep</u> wool _____

9. the <u>chicks</u> food _____

10. our <u>cow</u> milk _____

11. the <u>rabbits</u> food _____

12. the <u>donkey</u> stall _____

B. Fill in the missing forms of each noun on the chart.

Singular	Singular Possessive	Plural	Plural Possessive
13. fox			
14.		kittens	
15. horse			
16.			insects'
17.	duck's		

Name _____ Date _____

Focus on Pronouns

A pronoun is a word that takes the place of a noun or pronoun.
A pronoun can be singular or plural.

Singular Pronouns	Plural Pronouns
I, me	we, us
you	you
he, him, she, her, it	they, them

Long ago, stories explained nature. They told about it.

↑ replaces stories   ↑ replaces nature

Circle the pronoun in each sentence.
Underline the noun or nouns to which the pronoun refers.

1. The Greeks had myths, and the Romans learned them.

2. When thunder rolled, it would scare people.

3. Zeus and Hera were strong-willed, and they often fought.

4. Zeus shouted at Hera, and she screamed back.

5. According to a myth, it was the shouting that caused storms.

6. Mrs. Randall said she would read a book of myths.

7. "Are you going to listen?" Mrs. Randall asked Sonny.

8. Sonny said that he would enjoy hearing myths.

9. Storytellers were inspired by myths and often told them.

10. Meg read a myth that she liked very much.

Name _____ Date _____

Subject Pronouns

Some pronouns can be used as the subject of a sentence. Subject pronouns must agree with verbs. A subject pronoun can be used alone, with a noun, or with another pronoun.

Singular Subject Pronouns	Plural Subject Pronouns
I you he she it	we you they

Peggy loves apples. She picks apples at a farm.

↑ ↑

subject pronoun and verb agree

Phil and I help. He and I like apples too.

↑ ↑   ↑ ↑

noun and pronoun   two pronouns

Rewrite each sentence using a subject pronoun to replace the underlined words.

1. The <u>orchard</u> is on a big farm. _____

2. <u>Phil and Peggy</u> drive there. _____

3. <u>Jodi and I</u> take our bikes. _____

4. <u>Phil</u> gets baskets for the apples. _____

5. <u>Jodi</u> finds a ladder. _____

6. The <u>apples</u> look very inviting. _____

7. One large red <u>apple</u> falls at our feet. _____

8. <u>Peggy</u> takes a bite. _____

9. <u>Phil and I</u> begin to pick. _____

10. <u>Jodi and you</u> fill a basket quickly. _____

Name _____ Date _____

Object Pronouns

Some pronouns are used after action verbs or at the end of prepositional phrases. These pronouns are called object pronouns.

Singular Object Pronouns					**Plural Object Pronouns**		
me	you	him	her	it	us	you	them

Jude packed his tools. **He packed them.** **He had a bag and put his brush <u>in it</u>.**

action verb   object pronoun   prepositional phrase with object pronoun

Add the correct pronoun to each sentence.

1. Jude's friend Wendy called _____ about the expedition.

         him   he

2. Jude asked _____ to join the group.

     she   her

3. Wendy told _____ about this invitation.

     we   us

4. She explained to _____ what archeologists do.

     me   I

5. She respects _____ for their work.

     they   them

6. Jude and Wendy suggested a book about archeology for _____ .

     we   us

7. Victor thanked Jude for _____ .

     it   they

8. Victor will share the book with _____ .

     you   we

9. Jude is an expert, and the book is by _____ .

     him   he

Possessive Pronouns

Possessive pronouns show ownership. Some possessive pronouns are used before nouns. Other possessive pronouns stand alone.

Possessive Pronoun	Used Before a Noun	Used by Itself
my, mine	This is my bowl.	This bowl is mine.
your, yours	This is your bowl.	This bowl is yours.
her, hers	This is her bowl.	This bowl is hers.
his	This is his bowl.	This bowl is his.
its	This is its bowl.	
our, ours	This is our bowl.	This bowl is ours.
their, theirs	This is their bowl.	This bowl is theirs.

Circle the possessive pronouns in each sentence.

1. Bruce brought our boxes into his kitchen.

2. "My dishes will be different than yours," I pointed out.

3. "I will take the dishes that are mine to my house later," I said.

4. "Your friend has some plates like mine," he told me.

5. "Let's open this box of ours and see its contents."

6. "Are these bowls mine, or are they yours?"

7. Mom removed her teacups and some other things of hers.

8. She loved their pattern and its bright colors.

9. Bruce unpacked our dishes.

10. He stopped to admire my favorite pitcher.

11. "This is yours," he said.

12. Our grandparents left us many of their things.

   Great Grammar Practice, Grade 5 © 2015 by Scholastic Teaching Resources

Name _____ Date _____

Review: Nouns and Pronouns

A noun is a word that names a person, place, thing, or idea.

Nouns can be proper. Nouns also have plural or possessive forms.

A pronoun is a word that takes the place of a noun or pronoun.

Pronouns can be singular, plural, or possessive.
They can stand for objects or subjects.

A. Write an example of a proper noun for each common noun below.

1. city _____   **4.** mountain _____

2. month _____   **5.** author _____

3. holiday _____   **6.** planet _____

B. Write the correct pronoun to complete each sentence.

7. Letters arrived for both of _____ this afternoon.
    you   yours

8. _____ penpal lives in Naples, Italy.
    My   Mine

9. _____ is named Antonia, and _____ are the same age!
    She   Her   we   us

10. "Who sent a letter to _____ ?" asked Jason.
    I   me

11. _____ letter is from Arjun.
    Your   Yours

12. _____ lives in Delhi, India.
    He   They

Great Grammar Practice, Grade 5 © 2015 by Scholastic Teaching Resources

Focus on Verbs

Some verbs show action. Other verbs link the subject to a word
in the predicate. Linking verbs are forms of the verb *to be*.
Other linking verbs are *seem*, *feel*, and *become*.

My sister Gigi married Jason. They celebrated their wedding at our house.

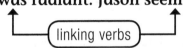

action verbs

Gigi was radiant. Jason seemed very happy, too.

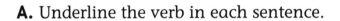

linking verbs

A. Underline the verb in each sentence.

1. Guests arrived from many parts of the country.

2. Everyone was happy for Gigi and Jason.

3. That morning the sun rose on a beautiful day.

4. The bride seemed very serene and calm.

5. I became a little tearful.

6. Gigi gave me a big hug.

B. Write *action* or *linking* to describe the verb in each sentence.

7. Cindy was one of Gigi's bridesmaids.   _____

8. She wore a long yellow gown.   _____

9. Gigi carried an enormous blue and white bouquet. _____

10. The guests threw rose petals at the couple.   _____

11. A wedding is such a delightful occasion.   _____

12. Gigi's wedding was a good example.   _____

Name _____ Date _____

Action Verbs and Direct Objects

An action verb is usually followed by a direct object. A direct object is a noun or object pronoun that receives the action of the verb.

Glaciers <u>move</u> heavy layers of ice over Earth. Glaciers <u>move</u> them.

action verb   noun as direct object   action verb   object pronoun

A. Underline the action verb and circle the direct object in each sentence.

1. Glaciers erode the base of mountains.

2. A glacier carries rocks across Earth's surface.

3. Sometimes glaciers carve wide valleys from the land.

4. In Norway glaciers create fjords.

5. In oceans pieces of glacial ice form icebergs.

6. Ships at sea sometimes hit them accidentally.

7. An iceberg causes serious damage to a ship.

8. Passengers photograph icebergs from a distance.

B. Underline the action verb in each sentence.
Write your own direct object for each verb.

9. Rivers and lakes supply _____ for people.

10. Fast flowing rivers carve _____ in the land.

11. Rivers sometimes cause _____ in the spring.

12. Engineers build _____ on some rivers.

Linking Verbs

A linking verb is followed by a predicate noun or a predicate adjective.
A predicate noun renames the subject.
A predicate adjective describes the subject.

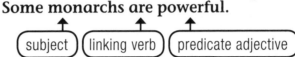

A monarch is a ruler.

subject   linking verb   predicate noun

Some monarchs are powerful.

subject   linking verb   predicate adjective

A. Underline the linking verb in each sentence.
Draw an arrow from the subject to the predicate noun.

  1. Henry VIII was an English king in the sixteenth century.

  2. Long ago in Egypt the ruler was a pharaoh.

  3. The home of a monarch is often a palace.

  4. The Forbidden City in China is a large palace complex.

  5. Some royal children became rulers in the past.

B. Underline the linking verb in each sentence.
Draw an arrow from the subject to the predicate adjective.

  6. The crowns of some monarchs were ornate.

  7. The Palace of Versailles in Paris is well-known.

  8. Hairstyles at some royal courts were extreme.

  9. Some rulers were very brave.

 10. Louis IX of France was very religious.

Name _____   Date _____

Subjects and Verbs

The simple subject and verb in a sentence must agree. If the subject is singular, an -s is added to the verb. If a subject is plural, the verb has no -s.

Chayo rides on a surfboard.   **The other boys ride too.**

↑   ↑

(singular subject; -s added)   (plural subject; no -s)

A. Read each sentence. If the subject and verb agree, write *agree*. If they do not agree, write the correct verb form.

1. The waves crash onto the shore fast and hard. _____

2. Chayo balance on his board.   _____

3. Overhead, gulls darts into the sea for fish.   _____

4. A motorboat bob on the waves.   _____

5. The clean sea air is bracing.   _____

6. A huge wave approach the surfers.   _____

7. The boys prepares for a long ride.   _____

B. Write the verb that agrees with the simple subject in each sentence.

8. Maggie and her dog _____ along the beach.

    jog   jogs

9. Maggie _____ a stick for the dog.

    toss   tosses

10. Some children _____ a big sandcastle.

    is building   are building

11. The castle _____ under a wave.

    disappear   disappears

Name _____ Date _____

Using Verb Tenses

Verbs can show action in the present, past, and future.
In writing, verb tenses should be consistent.

Present: The workers stop the truck.

Past: The workers stopped the truck.

Future: The workers will stop the truck.

Correct: They stop the truck and get out.

verbs are same tense

Incorrect: They stop the truck and got out.

verbs not same tense

A. Underline the verb in each sentence. Write *present*, *past*, or *future* to identify the tense.

1. The sanitation truck rolls down the street. _____

2. The driver pulls over to a curb. _____

3. Piles of garbage bags awaited pickup. _____

4. People placed these bags out the night before. _____

5. Soon the trash bags and recycling bags will be gone. _____

6. The truck will drop it off at the landfill. _____

B. Rewrite each sentence so the verb tenses are consistent.

7. A dogwalker stops and watched the sanitation workers.

_____

8. They hauled the bags to the truck and toss them in it.

_____

9. The workers hop into the truck and continued on their route.

_____

Verb Phrases

A verb phrase includes a main verb and one or more helping verbs.

Helping Verbs

am, are, is, was, were   has, have, had   can, could

Kendra and Stan are making a video.   **Amber is assisting them.**

↑   ↑   ↑   ↑

(helping verb) (main verb)   (helping verb) (main verb)

A. Underline the main verb twice and the helping verb once in each sentence.

1. They have worked all week.

2. Some classmates are acting in it.

3. Stan has scheduled many rehearsals.

4. Mrs. Blake is advising them.

5. Amber and Jada are feeling impatient.

6. Belle and Elijah are making posters.

7. Dora can develop an ad.

8. Everyone is contributing.

B. Write the correct form of the verb for each sentence.

9. We _____ a long time for the video.
        have waited   has waited

10. I _____ about it every day.
        is asking   am asking

11. Kendra and Stan _____ it for ages.
        has been planning   have been planning

12. For awhile the camera _____ .
        hadn't been working   haven't been working

13. Amber _____ pictures of the process.
        are taking   is taking

Using the Verb *To Do*

Some forms of the verb *to do* can be used as main verbs or helping verbs.

Main Verb	**Helping Verb**
I do my homework.	I do try hard.
Carl does his homework.	Carl does try hard.
We did our homework.	We did try hard.

The verb forms *doing* and *done* must be used with a helping verb.
The verb *did* cannot have a helping verb.

Carl is doing his homework.   We **have done** our homework.   We **did** a lot of work.

   ↑   ↑   ↑

(helping verb)   (helping verb)   (no helping verb)

A. Write *main* or *helping* to tell how a form of *do* is used in each sentence.

1. Carl and I did well on the quiz.   _____

2. We sometimes do our studying together.   _____

3. Carl did stay late at our house yesterday.   _____

4. We did math, science, and spelling assignments. _____

5. Carl does his reading homework in study hall.   _____

B. Write the correct form of the verb in each sentence.

6. I _____ some research about spiders for science.
          did   done

7. We _____ topics for our reports.
      did discuss   done discuss

8. Carl _____ a paper on gravity.
       doing   is doing

9. Our teachers says we _____ very good work.
           doing   are doing

Name _____ Date _____

Principal Verb Parts

The tenses for regular verbs are formed from the verb's principal parts. The principal parts include the present, past, and past participle.

Present	Past	Past Participle (with a helping verb)
play	played	played
taste	tasted	tasted
hurry	hurried	hurried
stop	stopped	stopped

A. Underline the verb in each sentence. Then write *present*, *past*, or *past participle* to identify the principal part used.

1. Tellers of tall tales exaggerate their stories. _____

2. Many listeners have wondered about tall tales. _____

3. American history has provided good sources for them. _____

4. Many unlikely heroes appear in these stories. _____

5. Dennis looked at some books of tall tales in the library. _____

6. The characters in tall tales stretched the truth. _____

B. Write the verb and verb part given in parentheses in each sentence.

7. Legendary heroes _____ daring deeds in tall tales.
   commit (past participle)

8. Tall tales _____ in the literature of many cultures.
   exist (present)

9. John Henry _____ on a railroad.
   work (past)

10. They _____ much laughter over the years.
   cause (past participle)

Name _____   Date _____

Perfect Tenses

The perfect tenses of a verb use forms of the helping verb *have* to show action. The perfect tenses are present perfect, past perfect, and future perfect.

Present perfect tense shows action begun in past and completed in present.	**Past perfect** tense shows action begun at one point in past and completed at another point in past.	**Future perfect** tense shows action begun in past or present and completed in future.
Our class <u>has picked</u> a field trip destination.	Our class <u>had researched</u> places for weeks.	Our class <u>will have enjoyed</u> three trips by spring.

Underline the verb in each sentence. Write *present perfect*, *past perfect*, or *future perfect* to show the verb's tense.

1. Our class has planned for the field trip. _____

2. For awhile we had worried about the weather. _____

3. Some students had feared a snowstorm. _____

4. The weather station had predicted a possible storm. _____

5. Now we have received good news. _____

6. The storm will have moved away by the time of our trip. _____

7. It will have drifted out to sea. _____

8. Teyanna has created a map of our route. _____

9. Zach had checked the distance last week. _____

10. The radio station will have prepared for our visit. _____

Great Grammar Practice, Grade 5 © 2015 by Scholastic Teaching Resources

Name _____ Date _____

Review: Verbs

> Verbs show action in the present, past, and future.
>
> Verb tenses should be consistent, and subjects and verbs in sentences must agree.

A. Write the correct form of the verb to complete each sentence.

1. In the city, people _____ the bus to get around.

take   takes

2. The bus _____ up passengers at the bus stop.

pick   picks

3. I usually _____ my seat to someone else who _____ it.

offer   offers   need   needs

4. My brother always _____ to push the button for the next stop.

want   wants

5. We will _____ the rest of the way.

walk   walks

B. Rewrite each sentence so the verb tenses are consistent.

6. The sun rose and the streetlamps will go out.

_____

7. The athlete warms up and began to exercise.

_____

8. Hikers walk along the trail and climbed over the hill.

_____

Focus on Adjectives

An adjective is a word that modifies a noun or pronoun.
An adjective tells what kind, how many, or which one.
Adjectives can come before or after the words they modify.

Cassie is thrilled with her new scooter.

     ↑   ↑

(modifies Cassie)   (what kind)

It is blue and has two streamers at the handlebars.

     ↑   ↑

(modifies pronoun)   (how many)

Circle the adjectives in each sentence. Draw a line from
each adjective to the noun or pronoun it modifies.

1. The shiny wheels of the scooter spin along the busy sidewalk.

2. Cassie is nervous as she navigates through the noisy crowds.

3. Her red helmet glistens in the hot sun.

4. She meets three friends near the big playground.

5. The happy pals set off at a fast pace.

6. With a mighty push, Cassie leads the laughing group.

7. The ride on the scooters is exciting and fun.

8. The scooter that Leon owns is black.

9. The riders zoom along on a winding pathway in the park.

10. They are breathless from the heat and exertion.

11. Cassie is thirsty and gets a drink of water at a fountain.

12. When they return home, the riders shout cheery farewells.

Name _____ Date _____

Proper Adjectives

A proper adjective is formed from a proper noun. Proper adjectives begin with capital letters.

Proper Nouns	Proper Adjectives With Common Nouns
India	Indian sari
Spain	Spanish olives
Canada	Canadian province

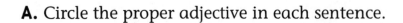

A. Circle the proper adjective in each sentence.

1. A popular dance in Ireland is the Irish jig.

2. Argentina is a South American country.

3. The Eiffel Tower is a French landmark.

4. William Shakespeare was an English writer.

5. Before going to Botswana, we bought a book about African animals.

B. Rewrite each sentence so that the proper adjectives are capitalized.

6. Some scottish musicians play the bagpipes.

_____

7. The italian language is spoken here.

_____

8. They sailed along the australian coast.

_____

9. They visited the egyptian pyramids.

_____

Articles

Articles are special kinds of adjectives. *A*, *an*, and *the* are articles. They are used before nouns or words that modify nouns.

Article Rule	Examples		
Use *a* before singular words that begin with a consonant sound.	a tree	a leaf	a gusty wind
Use *an* before singular words that begin with a vowel sound or silent *h*.	an apple	an honor	an eerie sound
Use *the* before singular and plural words beginning with any letter.	the forest	the air	the cool days

A. Circle the article in each sentence.

1. Ivy watched autumn leaves fall lightly onto the ground.

2. An easterly wind tossed them around.

3. The wind gave them an airy ride before it dropped them.

4. A gray squirrel scurried by looking for acorns.

5. Ivy wondered if summer had been an illusion.

6. Trees with bare branches now looked forlorn in the fading light.

7. Ivy picked up a yellow leaf and took it home.

B. Write *a*, *an*, or *the* to complete each sentence.

8. Jonas and Penny took _____ walk after lunch.

9. It was _____ crisp day in late October.

10. Now the sky was _____ unusual hue.

11. Was rain on _____ horizon this fall day?

Name _____ Date _____

This/That and These/Those

> This, that, these, and those are adjectives.
>
> | | |
> |---|---|
> | This and these refer to things nearby. | That and those refer to things farther away. |
> | This is singular. | That is singular. |
> | These is plural. | Those is plural. |
>
> **This** shirt has more spots than **that** shirt.
>
> **These** socks have more holes than **those** socks.

Write the correct adjective for each sentence.

1. The socks in _____ drawer are mine.
　　　　　　　　this　　　these

2. I haven't washed _____ socks over there yet.
　　　　　　　　these　　　those

3. _____ pile here on the dresser hasn't been put away.
　　That　　　This

4. These shoes have holes in the soles, but _____ shoes are new.
　　　　　　　　　　　　　　that　　　those

5. _____ pair in my hand needs polishing.
　　This　　　That

6. I will wear my blue socks today because I wore _____
　　　　　　　　　　　　　　　　　　　　　　that　　　those
red pair yesterday.

7. Does _____ pair of sneakers under the couch over there belong to Zoe?
　　　　this　　　that

8. Are _____ sandals the right size for me?
　　　　these　　　this

Focus on Adverbs

An adverb usually modifies a verb. An adverb tells how, when, or where an action happens. An adverb can come before or after the verb it modifies.

How: The puppy crept <u>quietly</u> under the table.

When: <u>Then</u> he put his head on his paws.

Where: He looked <u>away</u> in shame.

A. Underline the verb and circle the adverb that modifies it in each sentence.

1. Sometimes our puppy Fuzzy doesn't obey us.

2. That little dog races around in a tizzy.

3. He jumps energetically on chairs and couches.

4. Mom speaks sternly to the naughty puppy.

5. Yesterday, he escaped from the pen because of a broken latch on the gate.

6. We must take Fuzzy to a training school soon.

7. Fuzzy chews steadily on Dad's shoes and socks.

B. Add an adverb to each sentence. The word in parentheses tells what kind to add.

8. (where)   Fuzzy ran _____ when Dad scolded him.

9. (how)   The silly dog barked _____.

10. (when)   _____ Mom discovered one sock in the kitchen.

Good/Bad and Well/Badly

The words *good* and *bad* are adjectives that modify nouns or pronouns. The words *well* and *badly* are adverbs that modify verbs.

Anita took a bad fall.

adjective modifies noun

She needed a good doctor.

adjective modifies noun

Anita fell badly.

adverb modifies verb

She could not walk well.

adverb modifies verb

Write the correct word for each sentence.

1. Anita told Caleb the _____ news.
      bad   badly

2. Her foot hurt _____ from the fall.
      bad   badly

3. Caleb gave Anita some _____ advice.
      good   well

4. He told her to get some _____ rest in the coming days.
      good   well

5. The team needed her _____ in the track meet.
      bad   badly

6. Anita listened _____ to Caleb's advice.
      good   well

7. She wanted _____ to be able to compete.
      bad   badly

8. Luckily, Anita's recovery went _____ .
      good   well

Review: Adjectives and Adverbs

An adjective is a word that modifies a noun or pronoun. It tells what kind, how many, or which one.

Some adjectives are proper and must be capitalized.

An adverb usually modifies a verb. It tells how, when, or where an action happens.

Adjectives and adverbs can come before or after the words they modify.

A. Write the correct adjective or adverb to complete each sentence.

1. My grandfather liked to tell us his favorite _____ folktales.
   African   african

2. These belong to me, but _____ belong to my sister.
   that   those

3. The children splashed in the water _____ .
   happy   happily

4. We ate _____ pastries in Paris.
   french   French

5. The cat pounced _____ on the toy mouse.
   sudden   suddenly

B. Use the adjective or adverb in parentheses in a sentence of your own.

6. (good) _____

7. (bad) _____

8. (well) _____

9. (badly) _____

Name _____ Date _____

Focus on Prepositions

A preposition is a word used to form a prepositional phrase. A prepositional phrase begins with a preposition and ends with a noun or pronoun. The noun or pronoun that follows a preposition is called the object of the preposition.

Nine major planets revolve <u>around the sun</u>.   They move <u>around it</u>.

preposition   object of prepositional phrase

A. Underline the prepositional phrase or phrases in each sentence.

1. The solar system includes several kinds of objects.

2. The sun is a gigantic ball of hot gases.

3. Moons revolve around the major planets.

4. In addition to the sun, there are comets and meteors.

5. A comet is a celestial body with a cloudy tail.

6. Meteors are masses of rock or metal that fall to Earth.

Prepositions	
about	in
above	into
along	near
around	of
at	on
before	out
below	to
by	under
down	until
during	up
for	with
from	without

B. Underline the prepositional phrase in each sentence. Then circle the object of the preposition.

7. Mercury is the planet closest to the sun.

8. You could bake bread on Mercury's surface because it is so hot.

9. There is no water on Mercury.

10. Without water, there can be no life.

11. The planet Venus has no oxygen in its air.

12. Venus is closer to Earth than any other planet.

Name _____ Date _____

Using Prepositional Phrases

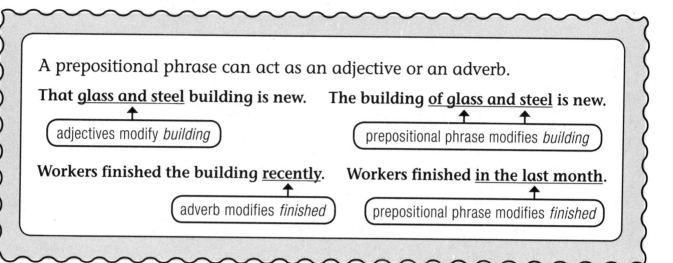

A prepositional phrase can act as an adjective or an adverb.

That <u>glass and steel</u> building is new.

adjectives modify *building*

The building <u>of glass and steel</u> is new.

prepositional phrase modifies *building*

Workers finished the building <u>recently</u>.

adverb modifies *finished*

Workers finished <u>in the last month</u>.

prepositional phrase modifies *finished*

A. Circle the noun that each underlined prepositional phrase modifies.

1. The walk <u>to work</u> is usually pleasant.

2. The architects <u>of the building</u> are proud.

3. The park <u>beside it</u> is also new.

4. Two women <u>with briefcases</u> approach the building.

5. Grace is the lawyer <u>on the left</u>.

6. A meeting <u>of employees and employers</u> will take place today.

B. Circle the verb that each underlined prepositional phrase modifies.

7. Workers ride the elevators <u>in the morning</u>.

8. They exit <u>onto different floors</u>.

9. Teresa Roma arrives <u>for several appointments</u>.

10. Manny Owen discusses building maintenance <u>with his supervisor</u>.

11. He walks <u>through many corridors</u>.

12. <u>At the day's end</u> he reports his findings.

Great Grammar Practice, Grade 5 © 2015 by Scholastic Teaching Resources

Focus on Interjections

An interjection is a word or phrase that expresses strong feeling. A strong interjection is followed by an exclamation mark. If the feeling isn't too strong, an interjection is followed by a comma.

Ow! That's my sore toe.   **Oops,** I'm sorry.

with exclamation mark   with comma

Oh no! You did it again.

phrase

Underline the interjection in each sentence.

1. No, I don't have it.

2. Wow! Look at my grade.

3. Aha! I've figured it out.

4. Whee! This is fun.

5. Ouch! That hurts.

6. Well, you didn't listen.

7. Say, that's great.

8. Ah, you are here at last.

9. Yes, I understand.

10. Oh, I misunderstood.

11. Right, I apologize.

12. Thanks! I'm glad you like it.

Whee! This is fun.

Using Interjections

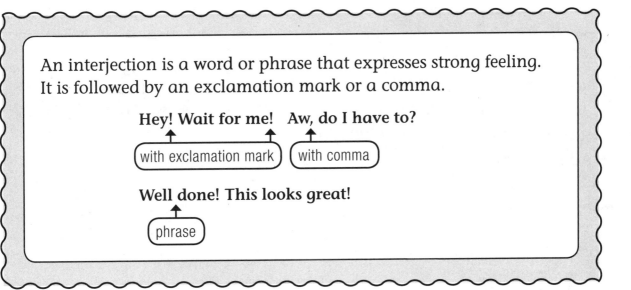

An interjection is a word or phrase that expresses strong feeling. It is followed by an exclamation mark or a comma.

Hey! Wait for me!   **Aw, do I have to?**
↑   ↑   ↑
(with exclamation mark)   (with comma)

Well done! This looks great!
↑
(phrase)

Use the interjections in the word bank to write sentences in each speech balloon.

WORD BANK

wow   goodness   sorry   stop   ugh   right

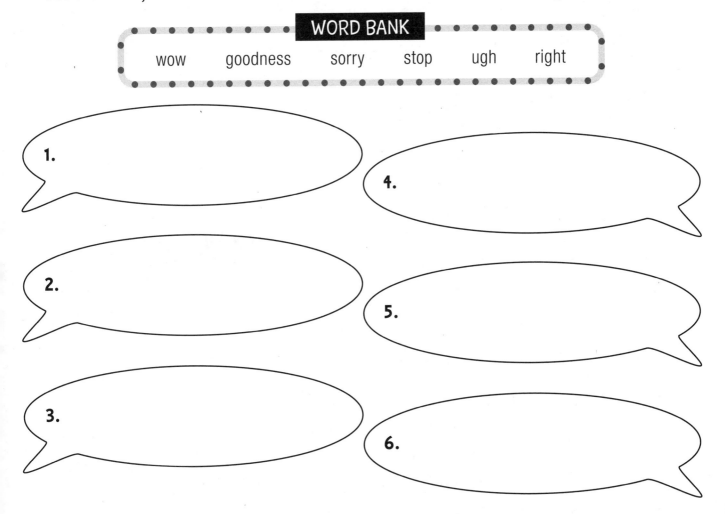

1.

2.

3.

4.

5.

6.

Name _____ Date _____

Review: Prepositions and Interjections

A prepositional phrase tells where, when, or how something takes place. It begins with a preposition and ends with a noun or pronoun. The noun or pronoun that follows a preposition is called the object of the preposition.

An interjection is a word or phrase that expresses strong feeling.

A. Complete each sentence with at least one prepositional phrase.

1. My family and I live _____.

2. We climb _____.

3. On Saturdays, I like to look _____.

4. I can see _____.

5. My friend waves to me _____.

6. I go _____.

B. Choose the best interjection from the word bank to complete each sentence. Use the interjections only once. Be sure to include a comma or exclamation mark.

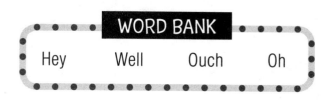

WORD BANK

Hey   Well   Ouch   Oh

7. _____ I stubbed my toe.

8. _____ I forgot to return the library book.

9. _____ Look over here!

10. _____ if you leave early, you will be there on time

Name _____ Date _____

Using Capitals

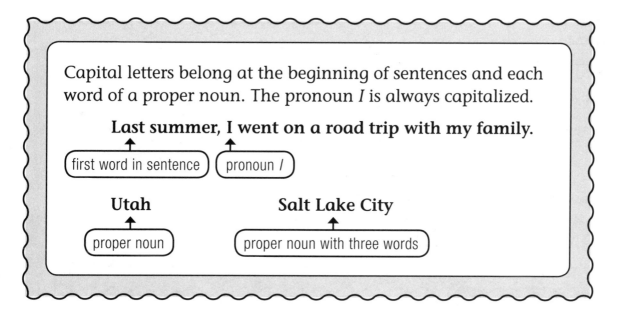

Capital letters belong at the beginning of sentences and each word of a proper noun. The pronoun *I* is always capitalized.

Last summer, I went on a road trip with my family.

first word in sentence   pronoun *I*

Utah   **Salt Lake City**

proper noun   proper noun with three words

Rewrite each sentence correctly. Be sure to use capital letters where they are needed.

1. mom and dad chose a destination located in the rocky mountains.

_____

2. we drove from portland, oregon, to yellowstone national park.

_____

3. yellowstone is mostly located in the northwest part of wyoming.

_____

4. its most famous feature is a geyser called old faithful.

_____

5. my sister jana had her camera ready when the geyser erupted.

_____

6. in september, i showed our photos to everyone in mrs. wilson's class.

_____

Name _____ Date _____

Commas in a Series

Commas separate words or phrases in a series. Use a comma and the word *and* before the last word in a series.

Pioneers in America crossed rivers, mountains, and plains.

commas separate words in series

Across rivers, up mountains, and over plains traveled the pioneers.

commas separate phrases in series

A. Add commas where needed in each sentence.

1. I've been researching pioneers: who they were how they traveled and where they settled.

2. I've learned that pioneers included hunters farmers and adventurers.

3. Most of them came from cities towns and farms in the eastern United States.

4. Pioneers traveled by foot on horseback and in covered wagons.

5. They were brave determined and hopeful people.

6. I'll go to the library after school on Tuesday Wednesday and Thursday to do more research.

B. Write a sentence of your own using all of the phrases in the word bank.

WORD BANK

long hours   endless work   many hardships

7. _____

_____.

Name _____ Date _____

Using Commas

> Use a comma after an introductory word in a sentence.
> Use a comma to set off a noun of address.
>
> | Comma Rule | Example |
> |---|---|
> | When you begin a sentence with an introductory word or phrase, use a comma to set if off from the rest of the sentence. | By the way, we are having a party.
As usual, I forgot to tell you. |
> | When you address someone by name you are using a noun of address. Use a comma to set off a noun of address in a sentence. | Eliot, can you come to our party?
Join us on Saturday, Eliot.
I hope, Eliot, that you are free. |

A. Add commas to set off introductory words or phrases in each sentence.

1. First of all we need to plan what food we will serve.

2. Well what do you think would be good?

3. Oh how about pretzels and popcorn?

4. Of course we'll want to have sandwiches and drinks.

5. Believe it or not Dad will make brownies.

6. Remember not everyone likes chocolate as much as you do.

7. Yes some people might prefer ice cream.

B. Add commas to set off nouns of address in each sentence.

8. Neil do you think we should have streamers or balloons for decorations?

9. I expect Emma that there will be music.

10. We are counting on you Eliot to be there.

11. Is this party for a special occasion Neil?

Writing Titles

Capitalize the first, last, and other important words in the titles of books, movies, songs, and other works. Underline titles of books, magazines, newspapers, plays, and movies when writing.
Use italics instead of an underline when working on a computer.
Use quotation marks for titles of stories, poems, songs, and articles.

Book:	<u>Julie of the Wolves</u>	**Story:**	"Sleeping Beauty"
Magazine:	<u>Cobblestone</u>	**Song:**	"Home on the Range"
Newspaper:	<u>The Lakeville Journal</u>	**Poem:**	"Casey at the Bat"
Play:	<u>The Lion King</u>	**Article:**	"How to Snowboard"
Movie:	<u>Star Wars</u>		

Write each title correctly. Use the chart to help you.

1. the phantom tollbooth (book) _____

2. ranger rick (magazine) _____

3. the sound of music (movie) _____

4. jabberwocky (poem) _____

5. the new colossus (poem) _____

6. much ado about nothing (play) _____

7. do you have healthy habits? (article) _____

8. los angeles times (newspaper) _____

9. america the beautiful (song) _____

10. little red riding hood (story) _____

 Great Grammar Practice, Grade 5 © 2015 by Scholastic Teaching Resources

Name _____ Date _____

Writing Dialogue

Quotation marks show the exact words that someone says.
Punctuation separates a quotation from the rest of the sentence.
A capital letter begins the first word of a quotation.

Position of Speaker's Name	Punctuation Rule
Before the quotation	Use a comma
Following the quotation (place this punctuation inside the end quotation mark)	Use a comma for a statement Use a **?** for a question Use an **!** for an exclamation

Pedro said, "The doorbell is ringing."   "Who is it?" asked Dad.

speaker   comma before quotation   question mark at end of quotation   speaker

Add quotation marks to each sentence.

1. Yoshi, tell me one of your favorite jokes, said Julia.

2. What years do frogs like best? asked Yoshi.

3. I know, said Julia. They like Hoppy New Years!

4. No, frogs like leap years, laughed Yoshi.

5. Oh, that was funny, Julia replied.

6. Julia added, I thought my joke was funnier.

7. Yoshi asked, Would you like to hear another one?

8. Of course, answered Julia. I like your jokes!

Name _____ Date _____

Review: Capitalization and Punctuation

Using capitals and correct punctuation makes a sentence easier to read. Remember to use capitals at the beginning of sentences and proper nouns.

Use commas to separate words in a series.

A. Add quotation marks and commas where they are needed.

1. We are having a canned-food drive next week said Mrs. Coburn.

2. How many cans should each student bring in? asked Sherry.

3. Mrs. Coburn answered Please try to bring in at least two cans.

4. I will donate five Sherry promised.

B. Write a sentence about your favorite book, movie, and song. Use the titles in your sentences.

5. (book) _____

_____.

6. (movie) _____

_____.

7. (song) _____

_____.

Name _____ Date _____

Easily Confused Words

	Confusing Words	Meanings
Some words look or sound almost alike but have different meanings.	accept except	to take other than
	exceed accede	to be greater than to agree
	affect effect	to have an influence on a result
	council counsel	a gathering to settle a problem advice
	principle principal	basic truth or law first in rank; a chief
	stationary stationery	not moving writing paper and envelopes

Write the word from the chart above that fits each definition.
Check your spelling. Use a dictionary to help you.

1. opposite of give _____

2. fixed in place _____

3. to cause a change _____

4. guidance _____

5. a notecard _____

6. same as *but* _____

7. to be more than _____

8. assembly that deliberates _____

9. an essential idea _____

10. a consequence _____

Name _____ Date _____

Silent Consonants

Two consonants together can stand for the sound of one consonant. The other consonant in the pair is silent.

kn sounds like /n/   knee   **wr** sounds like /r/   wren
mb sounds like /m/   limb   **gn** sounds like /n/   gnu

A. Write the word in each sentence that has two consonants that make one sound.

1. Greg knocked on our door this morning. _____

2. I was just climbing out of bed. _____

3. Zoe was in her room combing her hair. _____

4. Kelly was stretching her limbs in the hallway. _____

5. Mom was in her study writing checks to pay bills. _____

6. Dizzy our dog was busy gnawing on his bone. _____

7. Dad was in the kitchen wrapping our sandwiches for school. _____

8. Mom grabbed the knob and opened the door. _____

9. Greg handed her a bag of corn tied with a knot. _____

10. Mom said we would have the corn with lamb tonight. _____

B. Use a dictionary to find two words for each consonant pair. Write the words.

11. gn _____   _____

12. wr _____   _____

13. mb _____   _____

14. kn _____   _____

More Consonant Spellings

Two consonants together can stand for the sound of one consonant. The consonants *gh* together can be silent.

ph sounds like /f/ orphan   **sc** sounds like /s/ adolescent
gh sounds like /f/ cough   **gh** is silent   right

A. Write the word in each sentence that has two consonants that make one sound.

1. We talked with our science teacher after school. _____

2. We have been studying animals such as elephants in class. _____

3. When we present our reports, we will make scenery. _____

4. Omar already has his pencils, paints, and scissors ready. _____

5. Connie has cut out photographs of different animals. _____

6. One shows monkeys ascending a tree. _____

7. Another shows lions on the scent of some prey. _____

8. I hope my classmates don't laugh during my report! _____

B. Add a word spelled with silent *gh* to each sentence. Use the word bank to help you.

WORD BANK

high   sight   height   weighs

9. Elephants have the advantage of great _____ because they are tall.

10. If you ride on an elephant, you are sitting _____ off the ground.

11. Elephants are big; even a baby elephant _____ a lot.

12. From a distance, the _____ of a herd of elephants is amazing.

Name _____ Date _____

Prefixes

A prefix is a group of letters added to the beginning of a word. A prefix changes the word's meaning.

Prefix	Meaning	Example
over-	too much; above	overview
dis-	not	distrust
im-	not	impolite
mis-	wrongly	miscount

Underline the word with a prefix in each sentence. Write the word's meaning.

1. The library books are overdue. _____

2. We are lost because the directions misled us. _____

3. The painting was imperfect in some places. _____

4. If you leave the water running, the bathtub might overflow. _____

5. I dislike the taste of mayonnaise. _____

6. Sometimes, my brother will misbehave when Mom isn't looking. _____

7. It seems impossible to put this model together. _____

8. I hope they won't overcharge me for this comic book. _____

9. My twin sisters usually disagree. _____

10. Let's study our vocabulary words so that we don't misspell them. _____

Name _____ Date _____

Suffixes

A suffix is a group of letters at the end of a word that changes the word's meaning.

Suffix	Meaning	Example
-ous	full of	joyous
-able	that can be	likeable
-ish	having qualities of	pinkish
-en	made of	waxen

A. Add the suffix shown to make a new word. Write the word and its meaning.

1. marvel + ous = _____ meaning: _____

2. laugh + able = _____ meaning: _____

3. silk + en   = _____ meaning: _____

4. humor + ous = _____ meaning: _____

5. child + ish   = _____ meaning: _____

B. Complete each sentence with a word that has a suffix from the chart above. Use a dictionary to help you.

6. Something that is fun to do is _____ .

7. Someone who doesn't share is _____ .

8. This door is _____ .

9. Something like thunder is _____ .

10. This winter sweater is _____ .

Name _____ Date _____

Degrees of Meaning

Synonyms are words that have the same meaning. Among synonyms, however, the degree of meaning may go from not very strong to very strong. Choosing the word that shows precisely what you mean can improve your writing.

	good	great	super	amazing	
	1	2	3	4	

not very strong ⟵———————————⟶ **very strong**

Write a number under each word to rank the degree of its meaning.
Use the number 1 for "not very strong" and the number 4 for "very strong."
Use a dictionary to help you.

1.	unhappy	sad	miserable	inconsolable
2.	run	dash	race	jog
3.	microscopic	tiny	minuscule	small
4.	dreadful	terrible	awful	bad
5.	immense	huge	big	gargantuan
6.	happy	euphoric	thrilled	joyful
7.	weary	tired	drained	exhausted
8.	brave	fearless	heroic	courageous

Name _____ Date _____

Review: Spelling and Usage

Some words look or sound almost alike but have different meanings. Learning the meanings of these words will help you know how to use and spell them correctly.

Write the correct word from the word bank to complete each sentence. Check your spelling and use a dictionary if necessary.

WORD BANK

accept	except	exceed	accede	affect	effect
council	counsel	principle	principal	stationary	stationery

1. Inez was _____ when she saw the bear. She wrote us

on her new _____ .

2. How did seeing a bear _____ her? It had a strong

_____ on her.

3. The town _____ met to discuss this. A forest ranger

offered _____ on wild animals.

4. Did Inez's fear _____ the danger? Hikers should

_____ to safety rules in the woods.

5. Our school _____ spoke to us. Observe the

_____ of safety, she cautioned.

6. We must _____ the existence of wild animals.

They can be dangerous _____ in zoos.

Answers

Activity 1: A. 1. sentence 2. sentence 3. not a sentence 4. not a sentence 5. not a sentence 6. sentence 7. sentence 8. sentence B. 9. boys | stared 10. People | painted 11. cave | is 12. boys | accidentally

Activity 2: 1. Some **people** 2. Tall **buildings** 3. The **suburbs** around cities 4. Retired **people** 5. These traveling **homes** 6. A few Lapp **families** 7. The **Dayaks** in Borneo 8. About 90 **workers** 9. Many **kings and queens** 10. Village **houses** in Africa 11. A **family** with children 12. Common building **materials**

Activity 3: 1. **asked** her parents for a pet many times 2. **worried** about a pet in the house 3. **spotted** a poster about Adopt-a-Dog Month 4. **showed** the poster to her mother 5. **owned** pets 6. **kept** a bowl full of goldfish 7. **lived** on a farm with horses and cows 8. **suggested** a trip to the local pound 9. **could look** at the dogs there 10. **wrapped** her arms around her mother in a hug 11. **drove** to the pound the following day 12. **found** the perfect pet for the family

Activity 4: 1. interrogative 2. imperative 3. declarative 4. exclamatory 5. declarative 6. interrogative 7. exclamatory 8. interrogative 9. interrogative 10. imperative 11. exclamatory

Activity 5: A. 1. inverted 2. inverted 3. inverted 4. inverted 5. regular 6. inverted 7. regular 8. inverted B. 9. deer; are hiding 10. deer; step 11. dad; has fenced

Activity 6: A. 1. compound 2. not compound 3. not compound 4. compound 5. compound 6. not compound 7. compound B. 8. taste 9. boasts 10. get

Activity 7: 1. stands 2. are 3. have 4. are 5. is visiting 6. are learning 7. are making 8. changes

Activity 8: A. 1. compound 2. not compound 3. not compound 4. compound 5. compound 6. not compound 7. compound B. 8. Dad waxed the skis and checked the bindings. 9. They crossed the white field and skied into the nearby woods. 10. The snow crunched under their skis and sparkled in the sun.

Activity 9: 1. compound 2. simple 3. simple 4. compound 5. compound 6. compound 7. compound 8. compound 9. compound 10. compound

Activity 10: A. 1. sentence 2. run-on 3. run-on 4. run-on 5. sentence B. 6. Use a racket to hit a tennis ball. The ball goes over the net. 7. Runners do laps around the field. The track meet is next weekend. 8. The bus arrives from the other school. Now the meet can begin. 9. The runners cross the finish line. Jenna finished first.

Activity 11: 1. compound subject 2. compound predicate 3. compound sentence 4. compound predicate 5. compound sentence 6. compound subject

Activity 12: A. 1. socks 2. belt 3. scarf 4. musician 5. clerk 6. shirt 7. laziness 8. sweetness 9. fame 10. pain 11. confidence 12. bravery B. 13. Anna; clothes; winter 14. mall; father; jacket 15. pleasure; jeans; tops 16. excitement; Anna; boots

Activity 13: A. 1. jury; Mateo Garcia; October 2. time; courts; Greenville 3. prosecutors; lawyers; witnesses; court 4. Judge Coretta Kent; Monday 5. administrator; jurors; November 6. pen; neighbor; forms; Moses Young B. 7. common 8. Officer Wilson 9. Eastview School 10. Lake Michigan 11. Indonesia 12. common 13. common 14. Mount Etna 15. Minneapolis 16. Allegheny River

Activity 14: 1. essays 2. ladies 3. leaves 4. studios 5. wolves 6. churches 7. agencies 8. wishes 9. buzzes 10. circuses 11. classes 12. heroes 13. monkeys 14. calves 15. dishes 16. lunches 17. glasses 18. waxes

Activity 15: A. 1. dog's 2. children's 3. Thomas's 4. pigs' 5. spider's 6. bees' 7. hens' 8. sheep's 9. chicks' 10. cow's 11. rabbits' 12. donkey's B. 13. fox's; foxes; foxes' 14. kitten; kitten's; kittens' 15. horse's; horses; horses' 16. insect; insect's; insects 17. duck; ducks; ducks'

Activity 16: 1. them; myths 2. it; thunder 3. they; Zeus and Hera 4. she; Hera 5. it; shouting 6. she; Mrs. Randall 7. you; Sonny 8. he; Sonny 9. them; myths 10. she; Meg

Activity 17: 1.–10. Check that students rewrite the sentences and use the following pronouns. 1. It 2. They 3. We 4. He 5. She 6. They 7. It 8. She 9. We 10. You

Activity 18: 1. him 2. her 3. us 4. me 5. them 6. us 7. it 8. you 9. him

Activity 19: 1. our; his 2. my; yours 3. mine; my 4. your; mine 5. ours; its 6. mine; yours 7. her; hers 8. their; its 9. our 10. my 11. yours 12. their

Activity 20: A. Answers will vary. Possible: 1. Seattle 2. March 3. Easter 4. Mt. Hood 5. Gary Paulsen 6. Mars B. 7. you 8. My 9. She; we 10. me 11. Your 12. He

Activity 21: A. 1. arrived 2. was 3. rose 4. seemed 5. became 6. gave B. 7. linking 8. action 9. action 10. action 11. linking 12. linking

Activity 22: A. 1. erode **the base** 2. carries **rocks** 3. carve **valleys** 4. create **fjords** 5. form **icebergs** 6. hit **them** 7. causes **damage** 8. photograph **icebergs** B. Direct objects will vary. Possible: 9. supply water 10. carve paths 11. cause floods 12. build dams

Activity 23: A. 1. was; Henry VIII, king 2. was; ruler, pharaoh 3. is; home, palace 4. is; Forbidden City, complex 5. became; children, rulers B. 6. were; crowns, ornate 7. is; Palace of Versailles, well-known 8. were; Hairstyles, extreme 9. were; rulers, brave 10. was; Louis IX, religious

Activity 24: A. 1. agree 2. balances 3. dart 4. bobs 5. agree 6. approaches 7. prepare B. 8. jog 9. tosses 10. are building 11. disappears

Activity 25: A. 1. rolls; present 2. pulls; present 3. awaited; past 4. placed; past 5. will be; future 6. will drop; future B. 7. stops; watches 8. hauled; tossed 9. hopped; continued

Activity 26: A. 1. have worked 2. are acting 3. has scheduled 4. is advising 5. are feeling 6. are making 7. can develop 8. is contributing B. 9. have waited 10. am asking 11. have been planning 12. hadn't been working 13. is taking

Activity 27: A. 1. main 2. main 3. helping 4. main 5. main B. 6. did 7. did discuss 8. is doing 9. are doing

Activity 28: A. 1. exaggerate; present 2. have wondered; past participle 3. has provided; past participle 4. appear; present 5. looked; past 6. stretched; past B. 7. have committed 8. exist 9. worked 10. have caused

Activity 29: 1. present perfect 2. past perfect 3. past perfect 4. past perfect 5. present perfect 6. future perfect 7. future perfect 8. present perfect 9. past perfect 10. future perfect

Activity 30: A. 1. take 2. picks 3. offer 4. wants 5. walk B. 6. The sun rose and the streetlamps went out. 7. The athlete warms up and begins to exercise. 8. Hikers walk along the trail and climb over the hill.

Activity 31: 1. shiny, wheels; busy, sidewalk 2. nervous, Cassie; noisy, crowds 3. red, helmet; hot, sun 4. three, friends; big, playground 5. happy, pals; fast, pace 6. mighty, push; laughing, group 7. exciting, ride; fun, ride 8. black, scooter 9. winding, pathway 10. breathless, They 11. thirsty, Cassie 12. cheery, farewells

Activity 32: A. 1. Irish 2. South American 3. French 4. English 5. African B. 6. Scottish 7. Italian 8. Australian 9. Egyptian